O9-AIF-920

The Sound of MAD

Written by Nick Meglin

Illustrated by George Woodbridge

With no Foreword by Frank Jacobs

WARNER BOOKS

A Warner Communications Company

The SOUND of ONE HAND CLAPPING
for those who got me to hear it . . .
Stan and Joan Hart, Tom Allen,
Irv and Les Bernstein, Dan Fauci,
and/but, of course, Randy and Werner

WARNER BOOKS EDITION

Copyright © 1980 by Nick Meglin, George Woodbridge, and E.C. Publications, Inc.

ISBN 0-446-88844-3

Title "MAD" used with permission of its owner,
E.C. Publications, Inc.

This Warner Books Edition is published by arrangement with E.C. Publications, Inc.

Warner Books, Inc., 75 Rockefeller Plaza, New York, N.Y. 10019

A Warner Communications Company

Printed in the United States of America

First Printing: May, 1980

10 9 8 7 6 5 4 3 2

CONTENTS
The Sound of...

Foreword

To: Nick Meglin and George Woodbridge
From: Frank Jacobs

Dear Nick and George:
Sorry, but I can't come up with a Foreword for *The Sound of Mad*. I tried, really I did, but each time I couldn't get past the first sentence or two.

Just so you'll see that I *did* try, I'm enclosing all the Forewords I started but couldn't finish. Here they are—

☐ If you chuckled through *Crime and Punishment*, then you're certainly going to get a lot of laughs out of *The Sound of Mad*...

☐ A funny thing happened on the way to the *Mad* office. I saw Nick Meglin with his ear to a sanitation truck, listening to the sound of garbage...

☐ Four score and seven years ago...

☐ How do I love *The Sound of Mad*? Let me count the ways. Uh...

☐ The human ear is comprised of 31 parts, each of which is trained from birth to fight off wax...

☐ Call me Ishmael...

☐ Don't call me Ishmael...

☐ Because they have never been photographed together, it is rumored that Nick Meglin and George Woodbridge are the same person...

☐ Although *The Sound of Mad* is shorter than *David Copperfield,* it is probably funnier...

☐ Peanut butter, 2 qts milk, bread, 3 boxes Oreos, dozen eggs…
☐ When in the course of human events…
☐ Before you get into the fun part of this book, I think you should know that the pages are coated with poison…
☐ Books are great things to take on a vacation, and after reading *The Sound of Mad*, you'll need one…
☐ As Alfred E. Neuman once said, "Show me a trunk murderer and I'll show you a sloppy packer…"
☐ A long time ago in a galaxy far, far away…

So you can see I *did* try. Better you should get someone else to write your Foreword.

Sorry,
Frank

The Sound Of RADIO

Contrary to popular belief, there was a time in this nation's history when there was no TV! Honest! What kept people from jumping off buildings out of boredom, you ask? Radio, that's what. Radio offered a magic world, utilizing only sound to create "images" in the *mind's eye*. The following example will depict a typical mind's eye visualization...

Isn't she sweetness personified, Young Widow Brown?
SIGH
SMACK

Of course, that was only what you *think* you saw! What really took place in the broadcasting studio to create those mind's eye images looked something more like this...

THE SOUND OF WORDS

It would appear that many words and phrases are not used today in the way they were initially intended. Thoughts and feelings are added to what is being said in a way that often produces new meanings...

...as to my opponents charge that I'm a **"snob"** I can only say **au contraire!**

FRESH Although the *definition* of this word hasn't changed, the *meaning* has, as can be seen by...

GENIUS A word alluding to intelligence of oneself ("I'm a genius at math!"), someone you can take credit for being that way ("My son is a genius!"), or someone distant enough to compliment without comparisons being made to you ("Einstein was a genius!"). The word is *never* used in reference to marital partners or peers...

That John Blauner is a **genius!** He not only bought that stock when it was at its lowest price, but he held onto it when it went up, bought more when it slipped, and now took over as **controlling shareholder!** It's splitting and he's worth over a **million!**

Just a **roll** of the **dice!** He's **lucky,** that's all! Any of us could have done the same thing!

LUNCH A time of day used to achieve something other than taking food…

FRIEND This is a word suggesting a relationship that has too many interpretations to be clearly defined...

THE SOUND OF ADVERTISING

> Gentlemen, according to this latest poll, "honesty" is **in!** Is there anyone here who knows **something** about the subject?

Perhaps the most sickening thing about advertising is its *positive approach*. The con men and women responsible for magazine and TV ads never talk about their products with frankness. Rather than tell it like it is, they hide behind words and images in a way that insults our intelligence. Maybe they'd get more positive response with a negative approach...

WHAT HAS SHILTON DONE FOR YOU LATELY?

A lot! We've jacked up room rates—they'll cost you more than ever! So if you're shopping around for a hotel that's a bargain… just forget it!

Why? We don't want the penny-pinchers! We're after the snazzy spenders, the money crowd that flies first class and wears fifty-dollar shirts! At Shilton, you're going to pay through the nose!

Why, again? Because we offer fabulous rooms, snazzy towels, and snazzy people to rub elbows with, not your cheap tour groups and hicks with beat-up luggage you'll find in cheap hotels!

But, more important, these advertising campaigns
don't come free, either! We pay plenty for them!
And we pass that expense on to you! In spades!

WE GUARANTEE BAD BREATH!

Want to know why Ethnic National Salami tastes so good? It's the GARLIC we add to each succulent sludge of beef! Face it—you can't use pure, natural garlic without getting its pure, natural smell! And we're the first to admit it!

It Sure Does SMELL!

If you're after kissing-sweet breath, go suck on a mint! If you're after great salami taste, well, put off your love-making for another night and go chomp on a delicious and stinky hunk of . . .

ETHNIC NATIONAL SALAMI

WORTH EVERY SCENT!

SMASHED...
ON SEEGRIM'S V.O.

That's right.
Smashed.
First him, then his car.
And now he's one dead drunk.
Because he got tanked, polluted, sapped.
Which isn't what we had in mind.
We don't want you drunk.
We don't want you zonked out.
We don't want you bombed on the road and
  out of control and getting yourself killed.
After all—we're booze-makers, not undertakers.
We want our live customers—LIVE customers!
Losing drinkers can be the kiss of death for us!

SEEGRIM'S V.O.

This ad has been printed as a self-serving message

Most people don't seem to
recognize me anymore . . .

Either they've **forgotten,** or maybe they'd rather
pretend they don't **know me,** the effete rascals!

In any case, I used to be on magazine covers
and in the newspapers quite often . . .

And I hung around with **Frank Sinatra,**
Bob Hope and I did a lot of klutzy things . . .

The trouble is, whether they recognize me or not, they don't **trust** me! They won't even honor my **credit cards!** So the next time **you** get in trouble, make sure you have plenty of **cash** put away! **Cash talks!**

You're looking at the best camera in the world!

The LEIKON-FU

Sure you can't see it—we used it to snap the picture, silly! We're not like other companies who use OUR camera to snap pictures of THEIR camera for their ads!

Get the picture?

Get the picture! With a LEIKON-FU

At EX-RATED, We're Dirty!

Yeah, and our hands are black with grease, and our clothes are streaked with oil. But whaddya expect—Beau Brummell? This ain't no tea party; it's a service station, and ya won't find us on no "Ten Best Dressed" list when we're underneath your car and globs of gook are dropping on our face and transmission fluid is leaking in our hair!

If ya want a guy that smells pretty and looks clean—go to a country club!

If ya want a guy who'll make a mess of himself fixin' up YOUR car—act now: come to EX-RATED!

**Put a tiger in your tank
and a slob under your hood!**

It has been said that Alexander Graham Bell invented the "invasion of privacy." If that statement has a familiar ring to it, don't get hung-up over this next chapter...

THE SOUND OF THE TELEPHONE

Hello, operator? I just got a wrong number! No, not **this** time—this time I dialed **you** and I got **you**! It was the **first** number I dialed that I didn't get my party!

WRONG NUMBERS

ANSWERING SERVICES

Doctor Harkavy's office. No. the doctor isn't here now. This is his **answering service.** You can leave a message with me. Is that it? Just **that?** Two aspirins and lots of liquids will take care of that in a few hours! Listen, don't be such a baby! I mean, you should **hear** some of the things I hear all day! Talk about problems! Boy! Like, the call I got earlier today—this man gets on the phone, see? He's having a coronary, he tells me. A **coronary!** No one in the house! He's alone! It was tough enough for him to get to the phone and **dial,** I can tell you! I mean, **that's** a problem! What you got is kid stuff! Sure I took care of it! How? How else—you get the person to stop being a baby! **Stress** is what does it, you know! People **worry** themselves to death! I told him all about the phone calls I get from people with a lot **worse** problems than **him!** I told him to take two aspirins and drink a lot of liquids and he'll be like brand new in no time!

THE HUMAN APPROACH

Hi. You can't begin to realize how genuinely pleased I am that you called. It is communication such as this that brings about love, understanding, and the positve energy necessary for establishing and maintaining deep, personal relationships.—Unfortunately, I'm not home at this moment and so this message has been pre-recorded. Please leave your name and number and

And now,
NO word from our sponsor...

Do you know why you don't see many great silent film classics on your TV screen? No sponsors! They're afraid you'll just keep the sound off and not hear their marvelous commercials! Ahh, but what if some bright Madison Avenue ad man gets dialogue written for them so the sound *must* keep turned up? Here's what the famous "pay the rent—or else!" scene might look and sound like, shown at various viewing times with appropriate dialogue, when…

SILENT FILMS
GO TALKIE

(Or, "You're Still Better Off
With The Volume Down!")

FRIDAY MID-AFTERNOON—SOAP TIME

ARTHUR: *Rent is due on this typical Bronx apartment, Sadie.*

EARLY SATURDAY MORNING—KIDDY TIME

PETER
CHEATER: *Hi, Sillie Millie. I've got a great new game to play. If you win, you collect 200 dollars. If you lose, you go directly to "marriage". What fun! Now for our first question:*

LATE SATURDAY NIGHT—MATURE AUDIENCE TIME

FRANCIS: *I just paid up all the back rent due on this apartment, Cindy. That makes it MINE! You have to move out TO-NIGHT!*

FRIDAY MID-AFTERNOON—SOAP TIME

SADIE: *I know, Arthur, but let's face facts—I'm broke!*

ARTHUR: *But you make a halfway decent buck as a receptionist. Where'd it all go?*

EARLY SATURDAY MORNING—KIDDY TIME

SILLY
MILLIE: *I'm concentrating, Peter Cheater...*

PETER
CHEATER: *Good! What car has the largest TRUNK space?*

LATE SATURDAY NIGHT—MATURE AUDIENCE TIME

CINDY: *Why are you doing this, Francis? Just to keep me from marrying George?*

FRANCIS: *You've already GOT a husband! How many do you want?*

FRIDAY MID-AFTERNOON—SOAP TIME

SADIE: *With my father sick, I had to quit work to look after him. It's no joke, let me tell you.*

EARLY SATURDAY MORNING—KIDDY TIME

SILLY
MILLIE: *Gosh, I don't know. My father could help me with that one, but he's sleeping…*

LATE SATURDAY NIGHT—MATURE AUDIENCE TIME

CINDY: *Everyone knows I married old Sam here to cheer him up before he dies. This marriage doesn't count…*

FRIDAY MID-AFTERNOON—SOAP TIME

ARTHUR: *Well, my old offer still holds. As a slum lord, I haul in enough for you and me to live it up a little while we stash your old man in a nursing home!*

EARLY SATURDAY MORNING—KIDDY TIME

PETER
CHEATER: *Are you ready for the answer? It's "the Ford Elephant!" TRUNK space, get it? You don't pass go, you don't collect 200 dollars, but you DO go directly to "marriage!"*

LATE SATURDAY NIGHT—MATURE AUDIENCE TIME

FRANCIS: *I didn't come here to argue, sweets! Look what I took out today—A MARRIAGE LICENCE!*

FRIDAY MID-AFTERNOON—SOAP TIME

SADIE: *Thanks, Arthur, but no thanks. When Sadie becomes a married lady, it will be for LOVE, not money.*

EARLY SATURDAY MORNING—KIDDY TIME

SILLY
MILLIE: *I don't want to play any more games with you! You don't play fair. I'm gonna make fudge and you can't have any, so ha-ha!*

LATE SATURDAY NIGHT—MATURE AUDIENCE TIME

CINDY: *I'll never MARRY you!*

FRIDAY MID-AFTERNOON—SOAP TIME

SADIE: *And besides, I wouldn't marry anyone who isn't a PROFESSIONAL MAN!*

EARLY SATURDAY MORNING—KIDDY TIME

PETER
CHEATER: *Someone's knocking on your door...*

SILLIE
MILLIE: *I hope it's Willy Nilly, the new kid on the block. He's cute!*

LATE SATURDAY NIGHT—MATURE AUDIENCE TIME

FRANCIS: *Nor would I marry YOU, angel! Actually, it's for me and GEORGE!*

FRIDAY MID-AFTERNOON—SOAP TIME

SOLLY: *Hi, I'm Solly the doctor, Lena's neph-
ew!*

EARLY SATURDAY MORNING—KIDDY TIME

WILLY
NILLY: *Hi, gang! Got a question for you—what
new car has the SMALLEST trunk
space?*

LATE SATURDAY NIGHT—MATURE AUDIENCE TIME

GEORGE: *Forget it, Francis! I only went out with
you for your MONEY! But I've got my
own bankroll now!*

FRIDAY MID-AFTERNOON—SOAP TIME

SOLLY: *Heard your father was sick, so I brought over some of my aunt's chicken soup! And if THAT doesn't work, I write some pretty fantastic PRESCRIPTIONS! And here's some rent money, too! Am I not GREAT?*

SADIE: *A PROFESSIONAL MAN! Hoo boy!!*

EARLY SATURDAY MORNING—KIDDY TIME

PETER
CHEATER: *SMALLEST trunk space? Gee, I don't know!*

WILLY
NILLY: *The Ford Elephant COMPACT! Get it? I WIN, you LOSE! I collect 200 dollars, you go directly HOME, creep!*

LATE SATURDAY NIGHT—MATURE AUDIENCE TIME

GEORGE: *I got backing to open a hairdresser's shop, and Cindy here is going to be my manicure girl! So it's over between us, Francis! Take the money and run!*

FRIDAY MID-AFTERNOON—SOAP TIME

ARTHUR: *What chance do I have against a DOC-
TOR, let me ask! If I weren't such a
swine I'd sign petitions for SOCIALIZED-
MEDICINE!*

EARLY SATURDAY MORNING—KIDDY TIME

PETER
CHEATER: *Who cares! I break out when I eat fudge
anyway!*

LATE SATURDAY NIGHT—MATURE AUDIENCE TIME

FRANCIS: *Maybe had I used a different perfume…*

THE SOUND OF DIETING

There are millions of hungry people in the world. Don't be depressed—we're not talking about *those* kinds of hungry people! We're talking about the ones on diets! The *"Thin is In"* and *"Fat Ain't Where It's At"* people! It seems as though there are as many new, "miracle" diets on the scene as there are junk food places which create their need! Let's follow a typical case...

Hmmm, I need a scraper! Would you please look in that drawer next to you and get me a scraper?
Nothing here but an **apple pie**...
Acme
HAIR SCANNER S-210

Okay, how about the **wet diet?**
What's that?
Same thing in **reverse**. . . milk, no cereal! Butter, no toast! Mouth-watering, but no steak! **All the shampoo you want!**
Aw, c'mon. . .

Don't bet against gambling becoming legal—it's almost that now. With the government recognizing the loss in revenue it suffers by "turning a deaf ear" to what is probably the second oldest profession, it's only a matter of time when the sound of gambling will be heard everywhere...

THE SOUND OF GAMBLING

I consider the National Gambling Act a move for the **bettor**...

School Classrooms

Commemorative Stamps

ROLL THEM BONES!

7¢

HAROLD FORBUSHER ROLLS
23 STRAIGHT PASSES IN
BILL'S CLUB

ROLL THEM BONES!

7¢

BILL ROLLS HAROLD
FORBUSHER IN BACK
ALLEY AFTERWARDS

Reading Primers

See the basketball court.
See the people jammed in to see the championship game.
See the odds.
The home team is favored by 12 points.
Don't bet on it!
You'll lose! Lose! Lose!
See Dunk Cutely.
Dunk is the state's leading scorer.
Dunk can hit from anywhere on the court.
When he wants to!

Will Dunk score his usual 40 points today?
Don't bet on it!
Why? Why? Why?
Because Dunk is so good with a basketball he can also *miss* any time he wants to!
Without being obvious!
Obvious! Obvious! Obvious!
Today Dunk Cutely will be the game's leading scorer. Today Dunk Cutely will lead his team to the state championship. Today Dunk Cutely will make sure his team wins by *under* 12 points!
Shave! Shave! Shave!

MAKE 4 SELECTIONS THE...
BOOKIE OF

PHONE RINGS

DOOR CHIMES

IN COMES

COMPANY

NO STRINGS

GOOD TIMES

This unique approach to pony-playing allows you to place your bets weeks in advance of big races! No more traffic jams and mingling with losers at the overcrowded tracks! No more frustration of having a "sure thing" and no cash to back it up!

FREE WHEN YOU JOIN

THE MONTH CLUB

ROOM HUMS

REPEAT TITLE

GREAT SCORE

BY STEPHEN

As a member of BOOKIE OF THE MONTH CLUB, you just call your area representative and place your bet. You'll be billed at the end of the month if you've picked a few dogs, but chances are we'll be sending *you* some big bucks! Send in the coupon below and we will mail you the name and phone number of your Bookie of the Month. You are required to bet only 4 other races in the next 3 months to maintain your good standing in the club. After that, you may quit at any time—but by then you'll be a winner! And no one quits a winner!

While advertising is the art of selling products, selling "images" is another matter. People are sold to the unsuspecting public by another form of mendacity known as...

The Sound Of PUBLIC RELATIONS

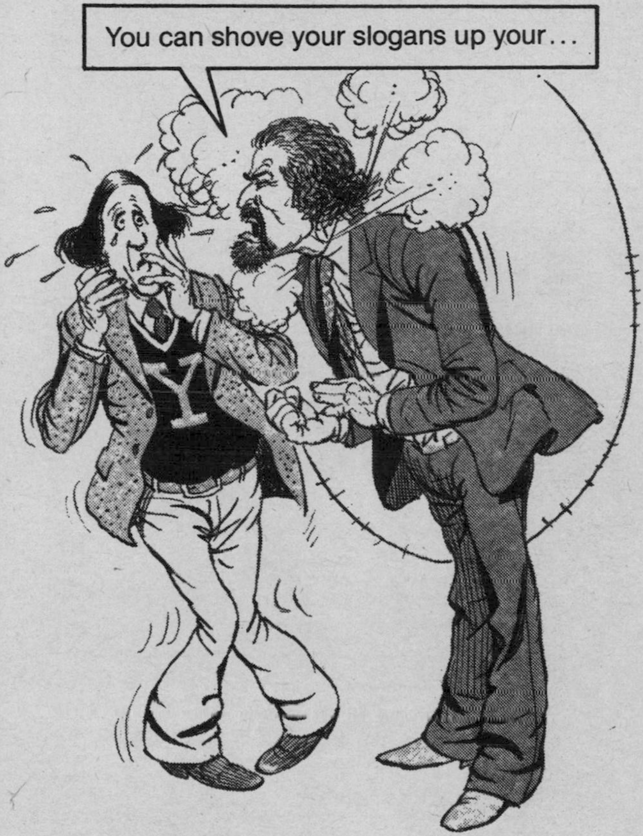
You can shove your slogans up your...

Good! Okay, men, let's call it a day! Remember, if we can pull this one off, it can take us **right to the top!** We'll have everyone who needs a new image coming to us—Howard Cosell, Gore Vidal, Norman Mailer, Reverend Moon, Billy Martin, Amy Carter, Philadelphia, Cuba...
TOTE
GW

There is a theory concerning relativity even more important than Einstein's! Everything is relative to each individual, which means that what's so for you isn't necessarily so for someone else. A joke, for instance, is funny only if *you* laugh at it—it's not funny if you don't, despite what others think. The following examples will seek to prove only one thing—Einstein's theory may be easier to comprehend than ...

THE SOUND OF RELATIVITY

SUBJECT: Drinking
ONE POINT OF VIEW:

I only drink socially! It loosens me up...

ANOTHER POINT OF VIEW:

He only socializes as an **excuse** to drink! And the amount he drinks doesn't make him loose— it makes him **stiff!**

SUBJECT: A Co-Worker
ONE POINT OF VIEW:

ANOTHER POINT OF VIEW:

SUBJECT: Leadership
ONE POINT OF VIEW:

Brent **thinks positive,** he always levels with you, he gives 100 percent all the time, and he's **not afraid** to make **un-popular decisions!**

ANOTHER POINT OF VIEW:

Brent's a **trouble-maker** who's going to shake-up everything and make waves! Just what we **don't need** around here!

ANOTHER POINT OF VIEW:

THE SOUND OF FOOD

As if the food served in some places wasn't bad enough, there is a trend of late to exploit the popularity of celebrities by naming certain sandwiches and dishes after them...

With or without **Debbie Boone?**
The Rock-Disco Room
menu
SIMON (PLAIN) 1.45
SIMON, WITH GARFUNKLE 2.80
DONNA SUMMER SALAD 3.50
JAMES TAYLOR, WITH CARLY ON THE SIDE 4.
ROD STEW 3.40
BEE GEES BURGER 2.95
BEATLES COMBO 12.50
RACHEL SWEET (9 FLAV .95
GW

We have become a society of statistics. The U.S. Government spends more money obtaining statistical information than any other government in the world! (It cost over 8 million dollars for the government to learn *that* statistic!) In recent studies, psychologists have found that people feel less alienated, isolated, hopeless, etc. when they learn they are part of a *bigger* picture . . .

The Sound Of
STATISTICS

IN 1980 THERE WERE OVER 10 MILLION TELEVISION SETS IN THE STATE OF NEW YORK

IN 1880 THERE WERE LESS THAN A HUNDRED!

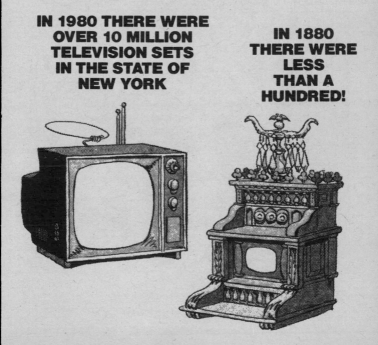

UNEMPLOYMENT

POLITICS

RELATIONSHIPS

STATISTICS, despite their *"figures don't lie"* acceptance, can, especially through "creative interpretation", tell stories of their own . . .

BIG BUSINESS

As Chairman of the Board here at International Dye and Rubber, I'm pleased to announce a **gain of 8 million dollars** this first half of our fiscal year over the last half of last year!

8,000,000

WHICH MEANS: ''We lost 47 million then, we only lost 39 million now, so we're up 8 million!''

Moreover, you could buy a share of our stock for **32 dollars 20 years ago!** Today, that **same** share is selling for **65 dollars,** more than **twice that!!**

WHICH MEANS: Inflation has given that 65 dollars a buying power of 14 dollars 20 years ago, so actually it's not worth even half of what it was really worth then!

SPORTS

You'll notice by the team's statistics that our time of ball possession was **36.2** minutes to the opposition's **23.8** minutes!

WHICH MEANS: They scored *quickly!*

WHICH MEANS: We "held" all right! Our statistics for *holding penalties* were tops in the league!

All in all, our **statistics** show we had a **successful** season!

WHICH MEANS: If you can forget one particular statistic — 2 wins, 12 losses!

JOB APTITUDE

You'll be pleased to know, Mr. Charney, that you're in the **top 10 percent** of the **lower 50 percent** in these aptitude examinations!

WHICH MEANS: Your low intelligence quotient insures your success as a creator of television shows!

THE SOUND OF TENNIS

There is nothing like the sound of a racket hitting a tennis ball! That famous "ping" has put the country into a racket sports rage! Now that we've established our flimsy excuse for including this chapter in our "sound" book, let's proceed with appreciation that it isn't a chapter about (yawn!) *golf*...

When he said I was **"no businessman,"** I let it go! When he said I had **"no sense of humor,"** I let it go! But when he said I had **"no backhand,"** I had no choice left to me but to **punch him in the mouth!**

EQUIPMENT

All you really need to play tennis is a racket and balls!
The *pro shops*, however, will try to convince you that
you need a lot more equipment to be successful at your
game. If they do convince you, they are successful at
their game! They already have a racket! This is known
as "net profits!"

Another consideration is how "tight" to have your racket strung. Even the novice should be able to spot a racket strung too tight or too loose...

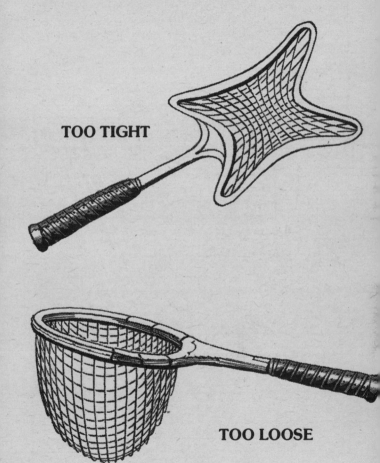

TOO TIGHT

TOO LOOSE

If financial investment is not a factor, you can give yourself an added edge by designing a tennis court that will favor you on your "home court." By tapering the dimensions slightly, your "side" will be slightly smaller, offering less area for you to cover and for your opponent to place his shots. *His* side of the court, of course, will be slightly larger for you to hit into and for your opponent to cover...

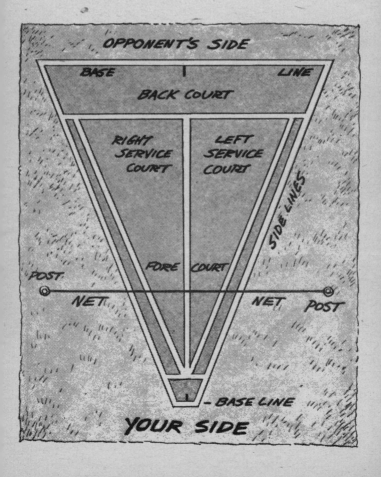

WOOD RACKET vs. METAL

The main advantage of a wood racket over metal is that a wood racket is easier to destroy in disgust. A metal racket will twist and bend rather than fall apart with that satisfying shattering, splintering effect that only a wood racket can offer...

SPEED AND QUICKNESS

A new can of balls, like a restaurant check, depends upon speed and quickness. By slowing down your approach, you can master the art of having other players open up *their* new can of balls before you open yours, enabling you to invest in just one can per season.

THE GRIP

There are several grips that all players must be familiar with before they go out on the court to make fools of themselves. Among the most popular are...

Eastern Forehand: Exactly as you might expect it would be.

Eastern Backhand: Exactly the same as the Eastern Forehand, only in reverse.

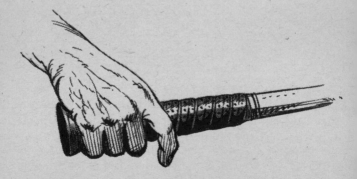

Western: If you are playing west of the Mississippi, you must use the Western grip. There is no difference between the forehand and backhand strokes, typical of Western thinking. It should be noted, however, that the Western grip is actually the Eastern if you are playing in Asia. In Israel, of course, the forehand is the backhand.

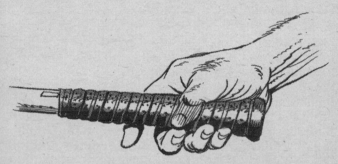

While the aforementioned grips are important to *improving* your game, they don't matter one bit if you don't learn the most important grip of all—*the finger pull and slash*—which occurs every time you have to open a new can of balls! It is used with profanity of the opener's choice.

How tightly do you grip the racket?

Bear in mind, too tight a grasp on the racket handle will result in a more "wristy" hit, which means little or no topspin and many shots going out. It is always better to grasp the racket more loosely.

How loosely?

My, but you ask a lot of questions! You should hold the racket handle loose enough so that it can fly out of your hand on a serve or overhead smash.
Why?
It's obvious, dummy—the opposition will be scared out of their wits when a racket streaks past their skulls, especially if you let it go early in the game. The rest of the game their concentration will be more on self-defense than the ball—a great advantage!

COMPETITIVE PLAY

While tennis appears to be a "gentleperson's game," it is just as cutthroat as any other competitive sport. How far someone will go in order to win is hardly discernible even on the "weekend hacker" level of play, and this approach isn't limited to the tennis court itself—the game is played at home, on the phone, and in bookstores...

STRATEGY

The best known tennis strategy is *never* playing against someone better than you! That reduces your chances of losing considerably, but not entirely, since you will probably choke at times that will insure your loss to worse players than yourself.

Very often, the margin of victory can be measured by a few lucky hits and some timely "bad calls!" A simple rule to follow is this...WHEN IN DOUBT, CALL IT *"OUT!"* WANT TO WIN? DON'T CALL *"IN!"*

CHARGING THE NET

After you serve two balls into the net, run up to the net quickly to pick them up and return to the baseline to prepare for your next double fault. By charging the net in this manner, you can speed up your game. That may prevent your opponent from falling asleep in the "ready" position…

DOUBLES vs. SINGLES

If forced to choose between a doubles or singles game, always choose the doubles game since having a partner to blame for losing is preferable than having to accept the responsibility for losing by yourself...

COURT ETIQUETTE

There are certain words or phrases used on the tennis court that distinguish the player from the slob. For instance, it is always polite to say, "Good game," to your opponents after you've smashed, slammed, and cheated your way to victory all afternoon. "Nice shot", is what is said after any ball hit to you, you flub. The shot itself can be a soft, ineffectual, easy put-away, but if you slop it up, cover up your inadequacies by acting as if the ball was more difficult to handle than it appeared! The same rule applies to receiving serve—anything you can't return is a "Great serve!"

EXCUSES

Probably the most important facet of the game is knowing how to minimize your inadequacies. Eliciting sympathy is one of the most popular methods of achieving this aim. You should spend a lot more time in front of your mirror perfecting your delivery of excuses than you should on the court perfecting your delivery of serve, since *you* will always do better with the former than the latter!

THE MEDICAL EXCUSE

This is a "no lose" situation! If he does beat you, he'll get no satisfaction—he's beaten an "injured" player. If he loses to you, his ego will be shattered forever, losing to a "cripple!"

THE PSYCHOLOGICAL EXCUSE

I just don't feel "up" today—the ol' killer instinct isn't there! The juices aren't flowing! As for the vibes...

If the opposing player believes this, he will undoubtedly ease off, figuring he doesn't really have to work hard to beat someone who feels beat already. Thus, he is vulnerable! If he thinks you are just trying to psych him out, he will work especially hard to beat you, attempting put-away shots and winners instead of just keeping the ball in play. The percentage is against him—he will thus psych himself out!

TENNIS LESSONS

Tennis lessons fall into two main categories—"con job" and "for real." *Con job*—The tennis pro suggests you get "screened" by one of his assistants to judge the present level of your game. If you are a woman, you get somebody like Lance Scorewell...

If you are a man, you get somebody like Chrissy Buttmaster...

For real—Should you be unfortunate enough to hook up with a tennis establishment that actually attempts to improve your game, you get somebody like Mark De Sade...

Racket back, bend your knees, get down to the ball, hit through the ball!

The lesson to be learned here is that sometimes being conned can be a lot more fun than trying to improve your ability at some silly game!

THE SOUND
OF
JUSTICE

PREPARING THE CASE...

DURING PLEA-BARGAINING...

HEARING THE TESTIMONY...

Of course, you never can tell how a verdict will turn out, but my guess is that we've just sewed up 8 "not guiltys" with our last witness!

THE SUMMATION...

...and please, ladies and gentlemen of the jury, don't be taken in by the facts presented by the prosecution! While I can't contest their validity, I can offer you an alternate perspective— The accused is a delightful fellow, fun at parties, and he has a warm smile! Aren't **these** important, too? Are we going to let cold, insensitive arguments affect our judgment?

AFTER THE CONVICTION...

MAKING A MOTION...

AFTER THE TRIAL...

Songs carry messages or, at least, attempt to. However, the messages usually concern love, lack of it, finding it or losing, needing it or ditching it, and other such nonsense! Of the *real* issues in the world—the problems, the future, the page one headlines stuff—nothing! Well, let's change

THE SOUND
OF
MUSIC

SEND IN THE CLONES

Sung to the tune of "Send In The Clowns"

Isn't it weird?
Isn't it wild?
My giving birth to a me—
I'm my own child!
Send in the clones!

Isn't it strange?
Are we a pair?
How did I get over here
When I'm still there?
Send in the clones!

Once I believed...
I was just one...
Trying to find my own space, my own place in the sun.
Knowing that I was unique...down to each pore;
Now I am *two*—
Or maybe more!

One is alone—
Two's com-pan-y—
And we all know that a crowd
Is made up of three;
But here come the clones;
We must stop the clones!
Don't bother—they're me!

WHERE HAS ALL THE POWER GONE?

Sung to the tune of
"Where Have All The Flowers Gone?"

Where has all the power gone?
No more gas - sing!
Where has all the octane gone?
There's no more flow!
Though I have a super car;
I know I can't go very far—
Pumps are dry at every turn...
Gas pains really make me burn!

Where has all the power gone?
Con Ed conned me!
Where has all the wattage gone?
There's no more flow!
"All-electric" is a mess;
When you sit there power-less!
There's no juice for me to use...
I'm about to blow my fuse!

Electric monopolies leave you with no alternate current!

Where has all the power gone?
Empty oil tanks!
Where have all those barrels gone?
There's no more flow!
Wintertime won't be a treat
'Cause I re - ly on oil heat!
And no crude has been accrued...
Or maybe we're being screwed!

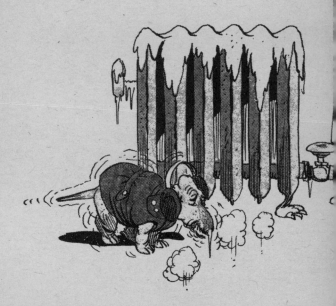

PORN FREE
Sung to the tune of "Born Free"

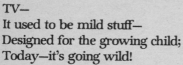

TV—
It used to be mild stuff—
Designed for the growing child;
Today—it's going wild!

Porn free!
That's not where it's at now—
To be a fat cat now—
Don't be...porn free!

THE SOUND OF SCIENCE

Sung to the tune of *"The Sound of Silence"*

Hello, progress—what is new?
Hello, advancement—how's by you?
Got lots - a fed - ral funds for trying
Some new 'lect - ronic ways of spying
As for cancer—it's just got to wait its turn
While we earn!
And that's—the sound of science!

Dreamed up ovens micro - wave!
Made processed foods the latest rave!
We don't care much about nutrition!
A starving world is not our mission!
There's no cash in ending hunger—so why try?
Let 'em die!
And that's—the sound of science!

BRAIN DOCS KEEP WORKIN' ON MY HEAD

Sung to the tune of
"Raindrops Keep Fallin' On My Head"

Brain docs keep workin' on my head;
'Cause shrinks know that guys like me will
    keep them all well-fed!
Eatin' up my bread!
Brain docs are workin' on my head—
    they keep workin'!
They just sit—it's like
    I'm talkin' to the wall!
I ask them why don't I take that bread
    and have a ball?
They said if I did—
Those brain docs quit workin' on my head—
    wouldn't need 'em!

That would mean I was cured!
A shrink knows it's a tip-off
When you flip-off—
And tell him you realize it's one big rip off!

Brain docs keep workin' on my head;
And I'm gonna go until my mind is fin'ly dead!
Then I'll be like them!
And start makin' some bread from each
    flake I'll be fakin'!
That's what I'll do—
I'll become a shrink, too!

BOAT SIZE NOW

Sung to the tune of *"Both Sides Now"*

Once a sports car rated high—
A status symbol you would buy;
Despite a price range in the sky,
It was the thing to do!
But now those wheels have lost their clout,
And what was *in* you find is *out*,
The time has come, without a doubt,
To change your point of view!
They judge you by your boat size now—
From aft to fore (that's stern to bow);
To make your image stay afloat
You have to have the big-gest...boat!

I recall another age
When super pads were all the rage;
Your living space the only gauge
Of how your status grew!
But now whatever pad you've had
Has gone the way of ev'ry fad;
The break you've spent—well, that's too bad;
Today there's something new!
You measure up by boat size now,
From portside aft to starboard bow;
The only way that you can gloat
Is when you have the big-gest…boat!

Dress yourself in fancy clothes
With labels that the *in* crowd knows,
And strike a fashion model pose
Like Pucci-Gucci-Coo!
But don't feel bad if no one stares,
'Cause status ain't what someone wears;
Those days are gone and no one cares;
The "best-dressed" phase is through!
They only look at boat size now;
If your yacht's got more beam to bow—
And if you don't you lose your vote!
You gotta get a big-ger...boat!

Daphne III